T0303663

Shadow Burn

Jordan Boyd

NOMADIC
PRESS

OAKLAND

111 FAIRMOUNT AVENUE
OAKLAND, CA 94611

BROOKLYN

475 KENT AVENUE #302
BROOKLYN, NY 11249

WWW.NOMADICPRESS.ORG

MASTHEAD

FOUNDING AND MANAGING EDITOR
J. K. FOWLER

ASSOCIATE EDITOR
MICHAELA MULLIN

DESIGN
J. K. FOWLER

MISSION STATEMENT

Nomadic Press is a 501 (C)(3) not-for-profit organization that supports the works of emerging and established writers and artists. Through publications (including translations) and performances, Nomadic Press aims to build community among artists and across disciplines.

SUBMISSIONS

Nomadic Press wholeheartedly accepts unsolicited book manuscripts. To submit your work, please visit www.nomadicpress.org/submissions

DISTRIBUTION

Orders by trade bookstores and wholesalers:
Small Press Distribution,
1341 Seventh Street
Berkeley, CA 94701
spd@spdbooks.org
(510) 524-1668 / (800) 869-7553

Shadow Burn

© 2020 by Jordan Boyd

This book was made possible by a loving community of chosen family and friends, old and new.

For author questions or to book a reading at your bookstore, university/school, or alternative establishment, please send an email to info@nomadicpress.org.

Cover artwork and author portrait by Arthur Johnstone

Published by Nomadic Press, 111 Fairmount Avenue, Oakland, CA 94611

First printing, 2020

Printed in the United States of America

LIBRARY OF CONGRESS CATALOGING-IN-PUBLICATION DATA

Boyd, Jordan 1986 –
Title: *Shadow Burn*
P. CM.
Summary: *Shadow Burn* is a journey through small, big lived moments of transformation. This collection of stories and city scenes is an exploration of now, then, and the spaces in between light and darkness.

[1. POETRY/URBAN LIFE. 2. POETRY/TRANSFORMATION. 3. AMERICAN GENERAL.] I. III. TITLE.

LIBRARY OF CONGRESS CONTROL NUMBER: 2019957648

ISBN: 978-1-7344377-1-3

Shadow Burn

Jordan Boyd

NOMADIC PRESS

for Joann and Christine

"Both light and shadow are the
dance of Love."

– Rumi

CONTENTS

CLASSROOM GUIDE

INTRODUCTION

The poems in *Shadow Burn* are the result of observation and contemplation on the many shades of light and dark in living. An attempt to know a little more the small space between the sacred and profane. An attempt to appreciate the small line holding together body and spirit, inhale and exhale, the ray of light ahead and the dark shape cast behind.

DIRTBOY

names himself
rib cage quiver
regurgitated elixir
and whimper at 8:12 am

as soul rips through his esophagus
into the porcelain bowl of water
past self and bile
and in that moment

he is

both
breathing and awake
perhaps even the two simultaneously

names himself
choke spit moan
slumped over the edge
and further in

as beads of sweat cascade his face
and a trembling palm pushes
down on a silver handle

water swallows all
bitter cringe dry heave shadow taste
and smoulder within

names himself
both
weight and porous
rebirth and vomit

ANOTHER HALLOW NIGHT

stumble south on High Street
the only plans tonight are to get fucked up a
nd pray together

stumble into the whispers
of good weed cheap vodka and orange juice
up rusted fire escape steps

as awkward shouts shape a one-person apartment
filled with the exhalations of eight
all strangers lovers and friends

half children
huddled together
for pointless intoxication

stumble towards the soft glow of another crooked face
deeper into the drunk high embrace
so bitter and honey

it is

the wandering mist taste of dancing in concrete circles
throat numb from cocaine and supplication
broken tongue vomit black saint recitals

we all hate certain days living
in Ohio
at least there are others

to swallow the smoke with tonight
to exhale self taste together
with gods that satisfy our half fallen plea

forehead bowing
towards the dirty wooden floor beneath

ALL TOMORROW'S PARTIES

all my friends buy weed
so we all buy weed from...
well let's just call him J
the best connection from here to unhinged doors

the thing about it is
J only comes into campus on Wednesday nights
so if you want the finest hydroponically grown in this scarlet grey city
you better be ready for the ceremony of anticipation

above the bar
six grown body boys and a tall art school girl in a one room apartment
pockets full of small earnings
we intend to exchange for an eighth of blue dream and shatter

the guy in the flannel tells the guy in the black hoodie
to turn up The Clash through the ripped speakers
then packs a bowl of crumbs
from the bottom of a ziplock bag

as they swallow the last drops of Kamchatka
chase it with water and growl
together on a Wednesday night
above the bar

in the sacred smoke of sharing
the last of what we have left

as J parks somewhere off High Street
and calls the one with the wanting eyes
to open the door to the second-floor stairs

ETCHED

1.

they don't really give a shit about your id at Bernie's
as long as you have enough cash and look kinda old enough

you can get a double rum and coke
for every body headed to the show for less than 10 bucks

as you can stand the smell of punk sweat spilt liquor
permanently etched into the black bar stools

on the other side of a black wood counter top
from a pale woman with a black tattoo

of a tree rooted from the thin outline
of the state you both settle into

and you say
I like your tattoo, that's cool

and she says
thanks

while you rip your glance away
together forever

and you carry three light brown drinks
to the table by the jukebox

2.

A Silver Mt. Zion acapella cut that man in two
as each arm you have is draped over
the shoulder of a shirtless friend

who swallowed two tabs with a double rum and coke

perhaps to know both skin and weightless
but that's so far from possible
it is true
days shorten so slow into tonight

can't even feel death load shadow cast
against the balcony beneath your feet
and the swaying shirtless bodies
under desperate wings

so slow didn't know it was a bass line cadence
cutting beneath the consonance
thought you were etched invisible everywhere
for a few measures

until you glance into the dilated void in another's pupils
bring your arms to your own side
and feel the weight of another man's sweat
cool your skin

GENTLEMAN

the concrete on the corner of Clinton Avenue and 4th Street
reminds his cheek of grandma's palm

skin cracked battered spit and walked upon
'til she solid and earth

caressing his squint face half-conscious reopening right eye
while a piece of dog shit glistens beneath street light blink

and a siren sounds somewhere through distance
as a Fela Kuti song leaks through silence

and he realizes
he is

and that the party is still going on inside
as he is one with the sidewalk

so he lingers a little longer with her touch
guesses horizontally at which song they will play next

and how it feels to have your shadow pull itself from your own open palm
as he heaves to his unstable stance and stumbles back into the house

on the corner of Clinton Avenue and 4th Street
to clean his face and drink more wine

DAVE

two men that used to live in the same apartment building
about three years ago see each other
in line at the White Castle on 1st and High

number 1 combo meal with Dr. Pepper asks small coffee with sugar
if he remembers Dave that used to live at the apartment

inhale

well shit he must have moved out before you got there then
you know I do remember now, he did move out before you got there
well shit you know that movie star Gwyneth Paltrow, right?
yeah man, Dave went to jail for stalkin' her
still in jail right now far as I know

exhale

yeah shit man
that's all he fuckin talked about was Gwyneth Paltrow
he just fuckin jacked off to Gwyneth Paltrow all the fuckin time
so shit man
he just went out to California one day

inhale

without fuckin' telling any body
went to her parents' house or some shit
and they busted him for that shit
put his ass in jail
yeah man
that guy was a real fuckin' idiot

exhale

two men grab extra napkins from the condiment stand
the night becomes 1:03 am

INQUIRY REPLY INHALE

almost last call siren
blast your bum face into next Tuesday
you want a bump?

so we off to the jigsaw tattoo walls with two empty stalls
and plenty of house keys to make into spoons
for small powder's silly balance

you think this suffering older than graves
or before that?

left nostril got a snap to inhalation
that make right nostril good jealous

yeah I hear the roof shingles rattle too
hope our shaman get this dream bang swallowed

before the urinal flushes a half-week's worth of sacrifice
with water and piss

as a quick sniff and rub
got all the answers

one breath closer
to the open door

FIRE WORKS

on the back balcony
on the third floor
on the brick edge

between here
and star dust swallow

as canisters fire crack boom
with humid July air

and the present time
concoction of chemical reactions
in receptors of mush

you lean over the edge
of the third-floor balcony wall

stare down into the sidewalk dance
pierced with afterglow explosions

calling come closer still

until you hear a friend say
look at those big red ones right there

and straighten your back
to see

the smoke
the fire
and shadow
of downtown

there for a breath
in one sky

THERE AGAIN WITH YOU

in a cheap hotel room off the Fremont strip
86 flyers for friendly women and prostitutes
are stacked against the lamp stand
as he walks around in his underwear drunk
shouting big exclamations

we're gonna get trashed tonight boys
gonna have some real fun
might even get my dick sucked by one these fine ladies here

while picking up a glossy postcard
then
a sudden dark tugs at the bottom of his lungs
says quiet while his bulge hangs over the foot of our shared queen-size bed

you know what guys
we're probably not gonna to be friends forever
I probably won't even know you guys a couple years from now

turns around and takes a big swig of Four Loco
and starts to put on his pants
as a reply goes

yeah we probably won't be friends a couple years from now

while a Steel Reserve pulls reverse from your lips with a sigh
and tilt your can towards his can

well let's get fucked together while we're here

and he picks up his can
thrusts it towards the space between

takes a big swig with eyes closed
puts it down
and goes into the bathroom shirtless

BIRD SANCTUARY

names himself
the observer

            or manifest
of space between shadow

                        light   question trail
                        between concrete   lake side
                        and bent tracks

names himself
a sanctuary of thin bone movement
against wind   and shit falling from sky
to earth   swallows everything
pushed through   or empty

THE EDGE OF A SOAP BUBBLE

everywhere night
bound to birth

dirt fight holy
fall fall and crash

no stars blink above our slab
of concrete east of downtown

must be christ or street-light flicker
got the space around
black majestic

broken tomb awaits the flesh you occupy
is that your sanctuary blood?
etched in slow crumble of polished stone?

got wings on a night heavy with flight
and that shit ain't nothing
but a burden most the time

the finest delicacy shit in reverse
yawns bring in oxygen
so does combustion

flame flame
smoke and burn
all symptoms between

MUSEUM DISPLAY

five weeks ago the dermestid beetles began to eat your flesh
first the soft jelly of eyes
then the mush of brain
and onto the trail of intestines

you were pulse mystery search dot
just five weeks ago
now the first meal for newly hatched larvae
as your skin dissolves into the pulse of exoskeletons

piling on the terrarium floor
your name now just jaw weight
for other black hungry dots
gnawing at the bone part still left of you

until that too is

FLAT SCREEN MAGIC

play magic when god devil me say
boy the entire interverse only a dial-up connection
until wish becomes flat curves flash
in a dark basement corner

breath slow watch itself
in   out
with the sound of the heater ducts

caught in the mystique
of there she is
naked alone

and we all
boy and mask girl
swollen blood rush and skin to skin
got alchemy in palm sweat

now watch this trick boy
take a black box
cold solid

twirl fingertips alone with every search
be majesty

BEHIND A CLOSED DOOR

he reaches for the door handle with his right hand
but sees something
there between the door and the tile

a space
and in this space
there is light
and there is dark

and somewhere never between or away
a shadow maker lives
and he sees a shape

so he pulls his right hand away
and steps back against the wall

and holds his piss a little longer
because somebody is in the bathroom

WE WINGS

only got this far south west by abandoning
to the behavior
of shattered paddle boats
in wave bang mist

fourteen steps from interstate 5
south of downtown steel glass
north of Chula Vista
in a shitty Eucalyptus grove

a red-black-white caterpillar seems to know
of something other
or at least wind
while eating into leaf

from branch
from sand
from shattered blue-sky vodka glass
cigarette filters and majesty

warm city breath against
the back of both your necks
seeming to know of something other
or at least wind

wings buried
somewhere in that shape
you are now

TRANSFORM BOUNDARIES

a lavender blanket drapes her right shoulder
as Al Green whimpers
so tired of being alone

left brain don't reach smile no more
but if it did she would ask questions
like if I ever feel any earthquakes out there in California?

and how often I remember
them tremors from the same
rock mass beneath both our small movement?

the second-floor room silent
'cept our breath exchange
and Al Green's pleas to a woman he squeezes himself to feel

she is here
and I am here
but she doesn't know it today

been on another coast so long I became mist
sharing the same room for the first time in months
and too much distance to feel my shadow

so this time
I stay for just a little while longer
to fall into the fault lines of her face

and guess at each story and aftermath
to hear ghost taunts
from her favorite song on repeat

sometimes late at night
I get to wondering about you
sometimes I hold my arms

as time between dusk and darkness shakes quiet the winter
I stand up
turn off the small cd player

say

good bye grandma
I'll see you whenever I'm back in town
okay?
okay?

kiss her on the cheek
as I become something mist
or less
her lips begin to tremor

BRAIN MUSEUM

1.

in cased beneath blink thin dust
her shadow artifacts display
as a lemon bar pulls reverse from my mouth

and her knotted knuckle palms press against the top of my shoulders
while Jeopardy answers with questions
on a small tv sitting on top of the microwave

what is remembrance?
when you are gone
and here together still we are?

beneath eyes shut and cracked sugar smile
at the kitchen table

as the microwave beeps three times
and I open my eyes

2.

and she answers with a mouth full of mash potatoes
what is forever gone?
when here you are now with me

at the kitchen table
together
with the divine burden of hunger

her long tongue goes out
much before the food is fully on her fork
and anticipation builds as the grey gravy and fluff

move towards her eyes open wide
to the extent of twitch at the right outer corner
a wide silver fork full of symbol and mush

sneaks toward her protruding tongue
eager to taste and swallow

as I close my eyes
when I hear the microwave beep

ON THE BACK EDGE OF HIS SEAT

he stares at the wooden floor beneath
as his blood shot eyes

paint ocean sunset wish
against Ohio winter wood grain

while sixties soul cd's and warm-blooded cocktails
surrender a bottomless canvas for my father never free enough

to roam far from Fair Avenue church bells
his bleach white dress shirt unbuttoned to his chest

hypnotized as Linda Jones and Gin
settle his wander starved glance

while holy ghost clouds
and two sons weigh his broad shoulders

heavy enough for double shots
his eyes half open closed

feet stretched out
stomach full with soul music and liquor

while his throat exhales
with the space between

THIS WATER BETWEEN

say
anywhere there is water
there is life

there is rise fall
gnaw away shore
land brave scar tissue

in low high tide tangle
say anywhere there is life
there is sorrow aversion crave

reason for syringes to slurp deflated balloons
as your voice quivers beneath a bridge
needle in hand

all those rivers away

STAIRS AND VOID

above the river
with glare towards the drishti of blue sky and shattered clouds
perhaps to avoid the black void below

calling come closer still

as I cross the most joyful needle's edge
on the jog around this small coastal town
blue sky reflects against water

which is not ocean
yet only small as distance
until it is so

so I run just a little faster to the place
where I return your missed call
so we can catch up and talk about the weather

you say man it's good to hear your voice bro
say it's raining hard in the heart of Ohio
been raining so hard it drips black tar

the color of your veins beneath a bridge
over the sinews of State Route 315
something like the color of water

beneath a narrow concrete pass over the intracoastal waterway
perhaps with no way to go but swallow
or pierce

and the counter melody of silence speaks for its time
as you are either sobbing
or singing too joyful for words

IN THE YELLOW ROOM

he might say
it is a late night in November
and this world is still here

and they have smoked about half an ounce by this point
one has a joint in his hand
and the other has a joint in his hand

both of them lit
yet they still reach
forth and back to each other's finger tips

to exchange the smolder
not for need
but because they haven't seen each other in months

A PICTURE OF US

wind strings minor tremolo the distance
as we sit two feet and oceans apart

on a seat with soft low tide sound
of some coastal state cold enough

to wear a sweater, jacket and baseball cap
beneath grey sheets of cloud

stories about our lives
we will never hear settle

as everything between us
is sea salt wind loud silence

there every time we sit together
in a picture of us

on this bench
at the beach

THE TEAM

me and he
watch the team war game
on a Saturday afternoon

fall full of leaf tumble on the world out there
while in here
the big screen tv in the basement booms play by play

between foundation pillars and hang on sloopy
as daddy low shouts
let's go

reclined as far back as the chair opens
with two slices of Papa John's on a red plastic plate
and a half cold Bud Light in a mug

me and daddy don't say much
just watch the game together
and hope our team can bring home a victory

ANY WAY THE WIND BLOWS

he's just a poor boy from a poor family
and I can't remember his name at all
just a few small gestures
between dark and light

the wink of a right eye
the sour pucker of thin brown lips
raised eyebrows as if question
with a pint of Jack Daniels

in left hand as he twists back
and my palm secures the half empty full bottle
as if to say
yes

I search for the calm in cringe as you
easy come
easy go
and yes

I do know some of the words to Bohemian Rhapsody as you
caught in a landslide
no escape from reality
slurring song in unison with the radio and a stranger

the right side of his mouth a little higher when he winks
whatever his name is
deep wrinkles around his eyes
from of all the nights we never knew each other

the glass bottle back against my puckered smile
singing the same words together as the air we breathe

I see a silhouette of a man
thunderbolt and lighting

NEWPORT AVENUE AND SHIRTLESS

you like to free style?
yeah I like to free style

I'll free style if you go first
so you free style first

there on Newport Avenue shirtless about 3pm on a Monday
you say something about seagulls on light posts that never turn off
he says something about sand clinging to bare feet
if only for a moment

a woman he can't find or forget
and he has this certain way of pronouncing the word home
more as if a question than a destination
he free styles

nothing of less
nothing of waves for shelter
he free styles
and you free style

and you hug each other
smile
and let go

FRIDAY AFTER WORK

man, fuck Wiz Khalifa's shitty ass music
but you know what
I would take a fuckin' bullet for that man though
because some of the deepest cuts I have shared breath with
have been because of that guys shitty ass music
living young and wild and free
my friends wrap their arms around each other tighter than last Friday
the living room of our mountain home cluttered
with PBR and shittier beer
leftover Napoleon Pizza and dried pine needles tangle the thin air
and she
dances as a skipping needle point
just having fun
and that's how it's supposed to be
if you asked me I prefer shit like
Charles Mingus
The Clash
Sun Ra or Coltrane
but so what
these are the times to put pretension aside
these are the times that sew spirit into bone
that remind just alive dying together
our ghosts burning into the valley
as she pushes repeat
we get drunk
we smoke weed
she stitches her shadow through me
as this shitty ass song plays one more time

THE LOBBY

the side eye angel of your face
passes through the lobby

as I breath we are love
in this moment

staring oddly towards each other for the first time
while a clock tick doesn't stop or start here

just makes another sound for the space we all share
between our rented rooms

as shadow follows your shape
until gone for that time

I am here alone
with the plastic flowers on the table

that will never live or die
until you pass through again on the way to your room

and this time
you don't look towards me at all

EXPRESS LANE 15 ITEMS OR LESS

on a Wednesday night beneath fluorescent moan
shadow jazz weaves through
each wound stitched back together

as they stare at small packages
her voice says
good   and you?

both their eyes glance
towards her hands and the other moving parts
as he wonders of the last time she felt her flesh scream

and kept breathing
dance guesses with her nametag
Jessica

and he knows what he would say
if there wasn't so much loud light between them
say it hasn't been so long at all

say he sees a scar on her right hand
hold that space together

as she exhales
and places a quarter and two pennies in his palm

ANIMALS

three guys cross 20th Street
one with a camera in hand
the other two in

black leather booty shorts
black leather combat boots
black leather paws and
black leather dog masks

the camera lens points in their direction
as they start to shake their leather squeezed asses
the way an excited dog would

then it gets real good
they start to wrestle each other
the way and excited dog would

or the way humans would
if they were filming a scene to a gay leather fetish porno
at Dolores Park on a Thursday afternoon

on the trim green grass by the children's playground
downtown erect in the short distance
the man with the camera says

bark
and they bark

wagging their black leather squeezed asses
as a small audience of seven or so

watch and wonder
if a dick is gonna come out

AGAINST LAKE MERRITT

do you think this is beautiful? see cause when I look at this
while pointing out at the low hill with one hand on her belly
it looks like a scar against the earth

you blink
and she is lying down in a black dress
with her lips against your tongue
on the low hill beneath the Fairy Land sign

as the office windows twinkle star night
and she caresses your left cheek with her index and middle finger
says

she wants to take her dress off
her skin is too close
and you

say
okay but they may be watching us from up there
pointing to space between light and dark

and she whispers into your mouth
it's too late night we are already here
you blink

open eyes onto the fog echo reverb against the bird sanctuary
and swisher sweet smoke between three circled bodies
huddled with silly laughs about the time of day

yeah she says
it's 3 pm and you can't even see the sun
and in reply to self

guess that's the way it is today
while exhaling lung ghost thick wind
it is nowhere but here

which is pretty fuckin shitty sometimes
and blink
hold to this here for a breath

until you hear
hey you dreaming or something?
and you say or something

as eyes open
and close again
towards the space between

WORTHY

we who are not worthy to receive angles
avoid the divine fragrance of god's semen manifest in the BART car

sitting at least three seats away from a woman who smells so human
it is a shame to stare upon our own naked filth

we swim in this shared moving
container soaked in holy aroma

waff together towards West Oakland station
with raised upper lip to nostrils

reminded of where piss and shit comes from
us too

and where it stays if you are so fortunate
we of little faith

take in soul motif through taste buds
and try not to gage on the paradise bouquet

as everyone breaths a little deeper
when the door opens
onto the next platform

FIRST FRIDAY

we who have spread our pores thin
through the work day week
for this Friday night on a chilled Oakland avenue
and the uniforms say silence

and in reply we raise 1 finger
shout rebel fury funk
shout foot stomp freedom
shout just to hear the lover in a stranger's voice

shout
1 more song
1 more song

and the dj shrugs his shoulders and points at the police
shout
1 more song
1 more song

all body craves aversion thump noise rare release
quiver cage against pulse
or ribs against heart beat
feet thrust against pavement as fingers point at hand cuffs

1 more song
1 more song

and the cop puts her index finger towards the dj
1 more

as Friday night swallows another morning

AT THE PEARLY GATES

Red say pray for me
Red say you ain't got a little more man?

in the last seven months touched a bed nine times
while holding up eight fingers

Red say no lie
you know I would help you out if I had it

Red say my own sister did it to me
Red say you don't know if the church is still open do you do man?

what time is it again?
the pastor said he would take care of me if I came back

Red say hey man
you can't help a brother out a little more uh?

while clutching a brown bag and sweaty metal can
face towards the stench of city

Red say you think it's gonna be cold tonight?
Red say ain't that some shit huh?

60 fucking years old and I got them bugs all over me man
and it's gonna be 75 bucks to get rid of 'em

while balancing between a black dress shoe and wounded sock
as a few more pieces of paper exchange grasp

and you both pass away beneath street light
and the dark spots between

WHAT IS LEFT OF YOU

stumble north up High Street
our prayers answered inside the walls of Larry's
that now exhales with clean corporate choices and large inches of flat screen

stumble by the black bar stools inside Bernie's
unetched into dust
and plastered back together into condos for freshman

at least Buckeye Donuts is still here
for now
a reliable place to get good cheap coffee
and a decent maple cream filled
and that one guy with the same name
and the same hat
still works here too
must be something to it for him
something that keeps him coming back when he could leave
perhaps
the repetition of shadow twist into slightly different shapes?
the faces red eye and familiar for a few nights?
the smell of coffee and fresh donuts?

as the door closes
and opens again?

EVE

three hours and forty-one minutes until midnight
tomorrow a new year
and there is enough cocaine here for everyone

snort jagged conversations on swollen couches
to share shadow with strangers
California girl clinks together two thin wine glasses

to celebrate another fallen year
as our reflections fade into the glass plate separately
and still   we smile

because we have found someone
to fall into the calm sea of connection with
if only for this crash wave shatter

drown into the freedom
of other frightened arms
inhaling deep the residue and ocean mist night

two hours and two minutes until midnight
California girl rubs her nose
and pulls palms towards closed door rooms

the powder fitting perfectly through a rolled ten-dollar bill
good lord
how the waves move in her eyes

all of them bloodshot
wide pupiled and wanting

one hour and fourteen minutes until midnight
University Avenue cluttered with divers and mermaids drunk as us
in search of calm in crowded lonely places

and if not for these other bent face reflections in cracked glass
what would we hold to?
as tonight decays between us

six seconds until midnight
tomorrow a new year
staring into the gray smoke wave eyes of California girl wondering

if I kiss you
now   here

will you float away
gentle into the sea with me?

ON BEAT

student asks teacher
what is shadow?
teacher say

                boom   bap
                boom boom bap

look momma I know how to drum
know how to burn past future 16th note matrix
with every odd 4th measure accented by 32nd dot fission

                boom   bap
                boom boom bap

floor tom say
e ah not quite mirror
without a misstep high hat

                boom   bap
                boom boom bap

& back beat just another sound to sky
while to the hands with loose sticks attached
it is breath

END BEGIN

this again every morning
or just when the rhythm gonna get ya?
whistle through reed and bend

silly masterful repetition
this here is the gate you are now
with sit twitch impulse a little longer than last urge

manifest maybe a smaller bright
pass through the shape of
who has control over so much yet nothing

this time an answer comes in an A sharp
finger back on that chord nameless or unknown
until spirit blow wind

call brass noise an answer with
the paradox of
silence an absence or every melody?

SIT FOR A WHILE

as the voice in the front of the room
mumbles something clear
about clapping or unwashed bowls

be settle in this
every need for something else
just that

face to face with ancestor and devil noise
in the space in between breath
only for that time

and this ordinary way sometimes shaped as agony
self dance both enlighten and dark cast against
and

sitting for just a little while longer
here
with that which is

ORIGINAL FACE

quick
before good or evil
what is?

somewhere between the tracks and concrete
for the guy in the flannel
and for the guy in the light gray button up

it's some where he hasn't swallowed yet
as his third glass of wine becomes
the story of when he did acid shrooms and suffocation together

and all he could see was mist in the shape of his mother's face
while breathless at the bottom of an empty river
says far back he can reach is screaming

inside an echo chamber
with a hand touching something not his skin
says maybe his shadow is too strong to reach that far back

it's just a paradox anyways
who may burn and watch the flame?
and the guy in the flannel responds

yeah man if you ever get the chance to try DMT
you should
but just so you know that's not where it's at either

but I don't know
I guess maybe it could be for you
and the other man's shifts into a flat smile

sort as if before good or evil
or before that
and then before that

says yeah
I might do that some time
as his face changes to something else

ON THE WAY BACK HOME

Ocean Beach
Abbott Avenue
about 8:35 at night

north of the thin concrete wall
south of dried dog shit piss taste
somewhere a little past the corner of Long Branch

this random guy shouts from behind you
ah man, you want a drink?
you stop and turn around

and he answers with a question
you know man?
a fuckin' Arizona Ice Tea or something from the store

so fuck it
go get a ginseng honey
and smile at him in his almost amethyst Chargers jersey

as he pays with a dollar and a dime
says
sure man it's cool enjoy your night

walks back onto Abbott Avenue
and goes north
at least for a little while longer

UNICORN THROW UP

twenty-three soft minds and restless fingers try to answer my question
what does abstract art mean to you?
and I realize this is a pretty tough question for third graders
so I show them a picture of Jackson Pollock's "Constant Change" again

say this is abstract art
so what does this look like to you?
and she shouts without hesitation
looks like unicorn throw up and I laugh

because constant change does look a lot like unicorn throw up on a canvas
so I say to them you know what
paint whatever you want and we are going to call it abstract art okay
whatever colors show how you feel

no boundaries
no limits
to you

but you better wipe up any paint
that gets on the table with a wet paper towel

8 ½ x 11 inches
frantic to contain the confusion
of childhood excitement and those rare circumstances
time is only felt when the bell sounds to go to your next class

and she rushes up to me
magenta smear and smile on her cheek says
Mr. Jordan I really like abstract art a lot
it's fun, here's something I made for you

and as she skips away through the four-corner door
I look at her picture
and it looks sort of like a unicorn threw up
on a white piece of paper

while through the window

sun   clouds   sky

burn above the blacktop playground

ON A NICE BACK PORCH

he got a tonic gin ice swirl in glass
on a nice back porch
what you thinking about?

ain't much to say
but this is nice
and let the stereo all that jazz

as both us close eyes with a saxophone solo
we can't finger
yet can inhale

and sip a bitter drink
and don't say nothing else
it just might throw off the groove we got here

AN AFTERNOON AND EYES

five chickens stare into the closed screen door
searching

perhaps for the man with the food
neck twists eye flinch and whistle

as river flows somewhere else
towards and away

from infatuation of that place
beyond the closed door

as the five chickens
begin to peck at clumps of dirt on the back porch

and at that same now
with an afternoon and eyes

a black white cat glares out the window
while atop a red table cloth

bird wing silhouettes twist neck twitch
it is

there
it is

here
and then it is

gone

the dance of self and shadow one
against the brick wall outside the window

as the cat begins to lick her paw
and look someplace else

COLD WIND CUT THROUGH

we who are not so accustomed to discomfort
in this fine city
cringe beneath a rare sky atop Park Boulevard

cold rain heavy against dusty concrete
empty 'cept one woman in a T-shirt
and I then remember Ohio

and one of the many reasons I left
what I cannot leave behind
that at times the air is so cold in November it hurts to breath

and you still keep breathing
only because there is no other choice but to breathe through this
and I then remember

one woman in a T-shirt
walking north on Park Boulevard

then some other direction
with arms pressed against her own weight

BURN AND SIMMER

from soil
root bloom through
all morning wind
on this street
reach north and south
chill bone run for it
right through bark and marrow
pulse spark
there was this one time
when we went through
frozen cut back towards
that other time
when you saw yourself
breath and fall onto dark
dense enough to rebirth so much give again
then this other time
a seed sprout through
crack froze numb dirt
call it stumble back to
as ether limps through parched lips
and warms the space visible above the morning
and sky with branches bare of leaves
all of them fallen
swallowed into
this burn and smolder
you both abandon and become

CLASSROOM GUIDE

Below, please find a few questions and assignments to consider when teaching or discussing *Shadow Burn*:

QUESTION 1

How is the process of growth and transformation (burning) observed in *Shadow Burn*?

ASSIGNMENT 1: Find two poems in *Shadow Burn* which illustrate the process of transformation from one state of being to another. Explain how these poems demonstrate "burning" and describe the two states of being that are revealed through the selected poems.

ASSIGNMENT 2: Write about the theme of "shadow" that is explored in *Shadow Burn*. What elements of the self does the "shadow" allude to? What elements of the human condition does the "shadow" allude to? Give at least two different examples from the book to help support your examination of the theme of "shadow."

QUESTION 2

How have you personally experienced transformation of your "shadow?"

ASSIGNMENT 1: Write two separate poems which demonstrate the process of burning that are based upon your personal experiences. Write a commentary on your own poems which explained how your were transformed through these experiences.

ASSIGNMENT 2: Describe what you would define as the shadow elements of yourself. Describe what you would define as the shadow elements of the human condition.

ACKNOWLEDGEMENTS

I would like to thank several groups of people who supported my learning-living process and development which is expressed through the creation of this book:

My family, including especially my mother, father, brother, grandparents, and Delores.

Close friends and companions who made the journey better by sharing together, such as Stephen, Joel, Ross, Edward, Nancy(s), Marolyn, Carly, Dante, Marya, Kristen, Lauren, and Annie.

Thank you very much to Cori Crooks and Hanif Abdurraqib for providing such valuable feedback on my manuscript.

Others who shared their impactful wisdom, such as Elaine, Ann, David, Hadley, Larry, Marley, Orion, Joanna, The Silver Oak Band, and Julie. I would like to also acknowledge all the other unnamed people, places, times, and breaths which influenced the creation of this publication.

Also a huge thank you to all those at Nomadic Press who helped make this book come to form. I would like to especially thank J. K. and Paul for allowing me to play music at their events, as well.

Thank you to the following publications, where some of these pieces first appeared: "Another hallow night," *Through Hell or High Water*; "Any way the wind blows," *Anti Heroin Chic*.

JORDAN BOYD is a writer, musician, and educator from Columbus, Ohio. Boyd graduated from Ohio State University and has taught and learnt throughout Ohio, California, New York, Spain, Florida, New Jersey, and currently teaches English Language Arts. Boyd enjoys jazz in the morning and blues at night. More examples of Boyd's photography, painting, music, and poetry can be found at *jordanboydart.com*.